D1064955

A LOOK AT YOUR GOVERNMENT

WHAT DOES THE US SUPREME COURT DO?

BY SANTANA HUNT

Gareth Stevens
PUBLISHING

CRASH COURSE

Please visit our website, www.garethstevens.com. For a free color catalog of all our high-quality books, call toll free 1-800-542-2595 or fax 1-877-542-2596.

Cataloging-in-Publication Data

Names: Hunt, Santana.
Title: What does the US Supreme Court do? / Santana Hunt.
Description: New York : Gareth Stevens Publishing, 2018. | Series: A look at your government | Includes index.
Identifiers: ISBN 9781482460599 (pbk.) | ISBN 9781482460612 (library bound) | ISBN 9781482460605 (6 pack)
Subjects: LCSH:United States. Supreme Court--Juvenile literature. | United States. Supreme Court--Rules and practice--Juvenile literature. | Courts of last resort--United States--Juvenile literature.
Classification: LCC KF8742.H83 2018 | DDC 347.73'26--dc23

First Edition

Published in 2018 by
Gareth Stevens Publishing
111 East 14th Street, Suite 349
New York, NY 10003

Copyright © 2018 Gareth Stevens Publishing

Editor: Kristen Nelson
Designer: Samantha DeMartin

Photo credits: Series art MaxyM/Shutterstock.com; cover, p. 1 jiawangkun/Shutterstock.com; p. 5 Gary Blakely/Shutterstock.com; pp. 7, 25 Everett Historical/Shutterstock.com; p. 8 Illegitimate Barrister/Wikimedia Commons; p. 9 Pool/Getty Images News/Getty Images; pp. 11, 13 Rob Crandall/Shutterstock.com; p. 15 Smith Collection/Gado/Archive Photos/ Getty Images; p. 17 UniversalImagesGroup/Universal Images Group/Getty Images; p. 19 Chip Somodevilla/Getty Images News/Getty Images; p. 21 (Supreme Court) Bettmann/Bettmann/Getty Images; p. 21 (Constitution) Dominic/Wikimedia Commons; p. 23 Paul Bradbury/Caiaimage/Getty Images; p. 27 Collection of the Supreme Court of the United States/Wikimedia Commons; p. 29 Paul Morgi/Getty Images Entertainment/ Getty Images; p. 30 Andrey_Popov/Shutterstock.com.

Printed in the United States of America

CPSIA compliance information: Batch #CS17GS: For further information contact Gareth Stevens, New York, New York at 1-800-542-2595.

CONTENTS

Words in the glossary appear in **bold** type the first time they are used in the text.

TOP COURT

The Supreme Court is the highest court in the United States. It heads the **judicial** branch of government. The Supreme Court makes decisions about whether government or state actions are faithful to the highest law in our country—the US **Constitution**.

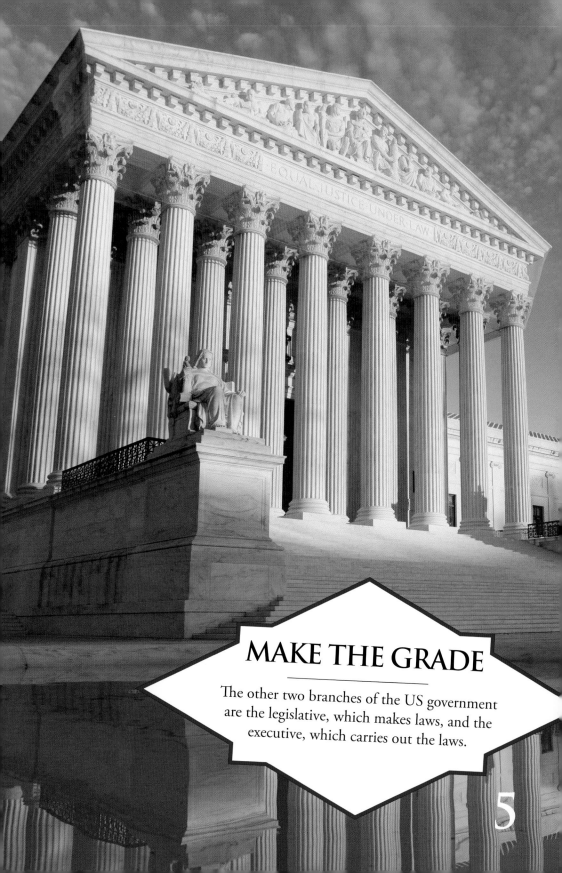

MAKE THE GRADE

The other two branches of the US government are the legislative, which makes laws, and the executive, which carries out the laws.

FROM THE CONSTITUTION

The US Constitution called for the creation of the Supreme Court. In the Judiciary Act of 1789, Congress set the number of people sitting on the Supreme Court at six. Those who serve on the Supreme Court are called justices.

MAKE THE GRADE

The Constitution gives Congress the power to create lower courts under the Supreme Court.

Over time, Congress has changed the number of Supreme Court justices through other laws. The Judiciary Act of 1869 set the number of justices at nine. That's how many sit on the court today.

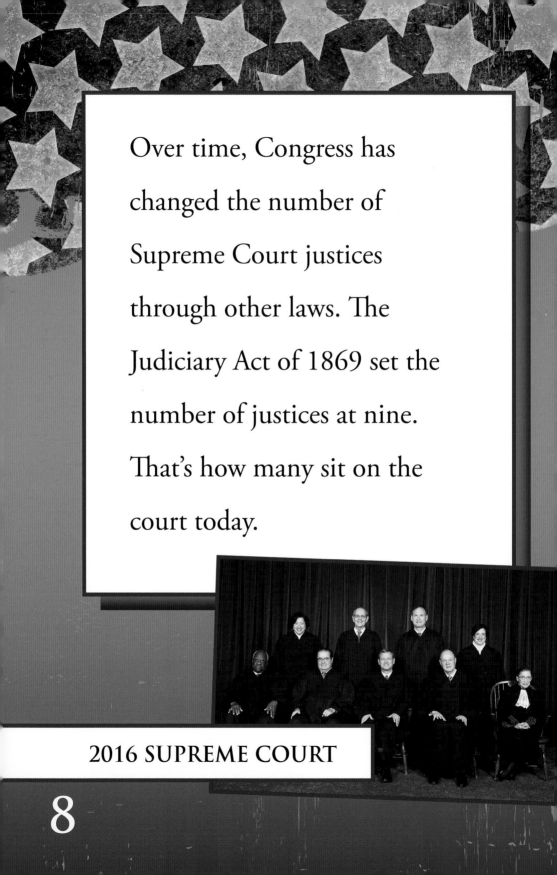

2016 SUPREME COURT

MAKE THE GRADE

One of the nine justices is the chief justice, who leads the court's business. The chief justice also swears in the US president.

THE JUSTICES

The Constitution doesn't give **qualifications** for Supreme Court justices. However, it's important that justices have studied the law. Today, most have attended law school and have worked as **lawyers** or judges.

MAKE THE GRADE

The Constitution does give qualifications for who can be the president or a member of Congress. For example, it says the president must be at least 35 years old.

11

The US president **appoints** Supreme Court justices. Though openings on the court don't happen often, the president commonly has someone in mind should a justice die or leave office. Both men and women can be justices.

MAKE THE GRADE

The president also appoints **federal** judges in lower courts.

JUSTICE RUTH BADER GINSBURG

13

Once a president appoints someone to the Supreme Court, the Senate must **approve** him or her. Senators look into the appointee's past and hold a hearing to ask him or her many questions. It votes to approve the appointee or not.

MAKE THE GRADE

The president appointing justices and the Senate approving them shows one way in which the three branches of government balance each other's power.

PRESIDENT RONALD REAGAN
AND JUSTICE ANTONIN SCALIA

15

A Supreme Court justice can serve for life. This means they can stay in their position as long as they want to. A justice may be removed by being impeached by the House of Representatives and found guilty by the Senate.

MAKE THE GRADE

To "impeach" means to charge someone in public office of wrongdoing. Only one justice has been impeached, and the Senate cleared him of the charges.

JUSTICE SAMUEL CHASE,
IMPEACHED 1805

17

THE CASES

The Supreme Court only hears certain kinds of court cases. It may decide what laws mean or how they should be carried out. It also rules on cases between two or more states.

MAKE THE GRADE

The Supreme Court hears cases between states and the federal government, too.

18

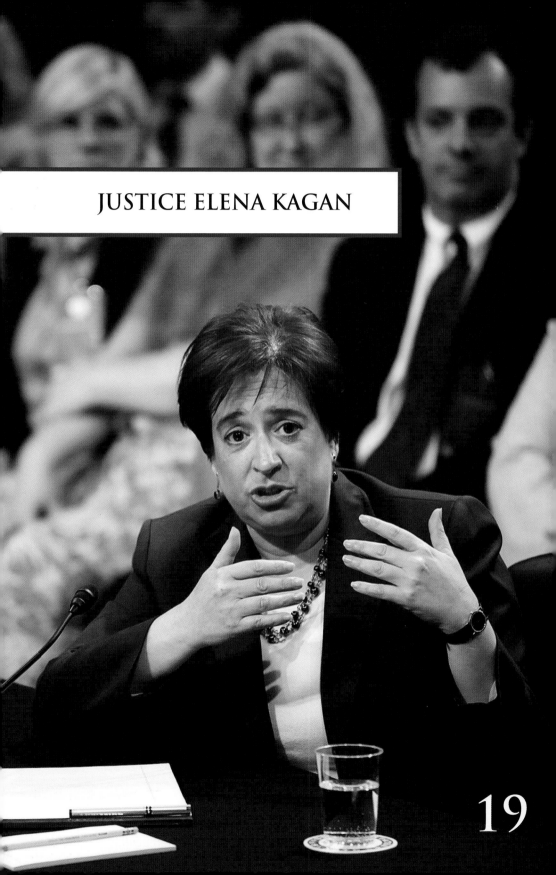

JUSTICE ELENA KAGAN

Most importantly, the Supreme Court decides whether laws or actions are constitutional, or faithful to what's written in the US Constitution. The ability to make these decisions is called judicial review. If a law is ruled unconstitutional, it's **repealed**.

MAKE THE GRADE

The Constitution gives US **citizens** certain rights. The Supreme Court makes sure laws don't take away or block these rights.

US CONSTITUTION

The cases heard by the Supreme Court have already been ruled on by lower courts. The Supreme Court has the final say. If the justices decide not to hear a case, the decision of the next highest court stands.

MAKE THE GRADE

Supreme Court decisions are like laws. After a ruling, the decisions must be followed.

BEFORE THE COURT

Each year, the Supreme Court hears about 80 cases. When a case comes to the court, the justices listen to arguments from both sides. They often ask questions. Sometimes, the justices hear many cases in a day.

MAKE THE GRADE

The Supreme Court turns down 7,000 to 8,000 cases each year.

The justices then meet to talk about the case. They don't always agree. When a **majority** is reached, the court rules on the case. The justices explain their ruling in a piece of writing called an opinion.

MAKE THE GRADE

Justices who didn't vote in the majority often write out why they disagree with the ruling. Their opinion is called the minority or dissenting opinion.

JUSTICE
ANTHONY KENNEDY

27

CHANGING TIMES

The Supreme Court sometimes overrules decisions by past Supreme Courts. This shows how ideas can change over time. New justices can affect the court's opinions, too. Even as it changes, the Supreme Court upholds the Constitution and citizens' rights promised in it.

MAKE THE GRADE

Supreme Court rulings are used in lower court cases, too. Lawyers use them as support for their case.

SUPREME COURT
FACTS

highest court in the United States

decides if laws or actions are constitutional

justices serve for life

nine justices including one chief justice

rules on cases between states

created by the US Constitution

GLOSSARY

appoint: to choose for a government office

approve: to officially agree

citizen: someone who lives in a country legally and has certain rights

constitution: the basic laws by which a country or state is governed

federal: having to do with the national government

judicial: having to do with courts of law and judges

lawyer: someone whose job it is to help people with their questions and problems with the law

majority: a number greater than half of the total

qualification: a feature that makes someone fit for a position

repeal: to do away with

FOR MORE INFORMATION

BOOKS

Loria, Laura. *What Is the Judicial Branch?* New York, NY: Britannica Educational Publishing, 2016.

Roland, James. *Ruth Bader Ginsburg: Iconic Supreme Court Justice.* Minneapolis, MN: Lerner Publications, 2016.

WEBSITES

Three Branches of Government

kids.usa.gov/three-branches-of-government/index.shtml

Find out how the three branches of the US government work together.

Publisher's note to educators and parents: Our editors have carefully reviewed these websites to ensure that they are suitable for students. Many websites change frequently, however, and we cannot guarantee that a site's future contents will continue to meet our high standards of quality and educational value. Be advised that students should be closely supervised whenever they access the Internet.

INDEX